TO:
DANIEL & Ch

Blessings on your
Journey!

Rev. Dr. A Foster

"So, You Say You Want to Get Married?

Now What"

By: The Reverend Dr. Andrew L. Foster, III.

Forward by: Lady Lorraine Foster

Order this book online at www.trafford.com
or email orders@trafford.com

Most Trafford titles are also available at major online book retailers.

Printed in Victoria, BC, Canada.

ISBN: 978-1-4269-2136-0

Our mission is to efficiently provide the world's finest, most comprehensive book publishing
service, enabling every author to experience success. To find out how to publish your
book, your way, and have it available worldwide, visit us online at www.trafford.com

Trafford rev. 11/06/2009

 www.trafford.com

North America & international
toll-free: 1 888 232 4444 (USA & Canada)
phone: 250 383 6864 ♦ fax: 812 355 4082

DEDICATION

This book is dedicated to all the strong, healthy marriages my wife Lorraine and I have seen modeled in our twenty plus years of marriage.

I am indeed grateful to Drs. Carol and Peter Schreck and Dr. S. Timothy Pretz for their untiring efforts and support demonstrated during the Doctoral Program in Marriage and Family Counseling at Palmer Theological Seminary. A special thanks to Dr. Alfred S. Maloney and Mrs. Gloria Maloney for serving as our clergy mentor couple.

Finally, to My Lovely Wife Lorraine,
You will always be the miracle whip on my sandwich, the salsa on my tortilla chips, the butter in my cake (no substitutes will do), the woman that God blessed me with to fill the hole in my very soul; you will always be my one and only lady; For Always!

- Andrew

FORWARD

At a certain age most little girls dream of getting married or have an idea in her head that she would like to get married and what kind of wedding she would like. Some play dress-up and house. Some even have a mock/play wedding ceremony with her friends. Dreaming of getting married and getting married is entirely two different events. One is a fantasy while the other is reality.

Many people go into marriage without fully knowing the person. Some enter marriage by their feelings, some were coerced, some thought they did not have a choice; some got married because they were pregnant, some for money. Not many actually thought of it thoroughly.

Before going further, let's look at some of the steps one must take before entertaining the idea of marriage. He's smooth; he looks good – well dressed. He's polite and well-bread; he is well mannered, he talks a good talk and has the right answers for just about everything. But is he the right person for you. Is this the real person, or is it just a show?

First you must know what kind of husband you want. Be

specific, the Bible says to write down your request and make it plain. So, write down all the qualities you would like in a husband. Write down all your thoughts, desires, and expectations.

Here are some examples of questions you can ask. Remember you don't have to ask the entire list at one time; and definitely not on the first date/meeting. Be realistic and be prepared for the answers you will receive. Don't accept vague answers.

- Is he a good provider – which means having a job that will provide for you and the children?
- Does he like children/want to have any?
- How is his health – sickness, disease, and family health concerns?
- How is his finance – Is he in bankruptcy, does he have bad/good credit?
- Is he a shopaholic – does he spend a lot on clothes, gadgets?
- What are his goals for the future?
- Is family important to him?
- Is he a Christian, Muslim, atheist, agnostic, catholic; you could be unequally yoked if you both don't share the same faith?
- What faith will the children (if any) be raised?
- Does he cook/clean?
- Who will be handling the finances?
- Does he have a child or children?
- How close is he with the child(ren)'s mother?
- Is he paying child support? – this will affect the budget in your household if you get married to this person.

Once you have gathered the information you must then ask yourself if you can live with any of the things on your list. Go over the list several times and be willing to change a few things, realize that you will not find everything in one person. Know that this person will not be perfect, and neither are you, but you must go into marriage with your eyes wide open. If you are planning on building a life with this person then you must know the "real" person. Nothing about this person should be a surprise on your wedding day.

Are you willing to give something up? Are you willing to negotiate or compromise something on your list? Once you are married and he starts showing signs of something you have on or not on the list, don't act surprised and say, "I didn't know this about you."

Enter this marriage with as much information about this person as you can. When you are finally asked the "big" question, "will you marry me" then you can give a resounding "yes," or "not right now" based upon what you know/discover about this person. I recommend that you not "rush" into marriage. There is so much more to marriage than a "feeling" and so much more than just the wedding day. Once the wedding day is over the real test begins. Will you be able to endure the test? With God's help you can.

Begin your marriage with love and prayers. So spend a considerable amount of time with the person before you say "yes" God has given you a spirit inside to guide you, so use it, and ask God if this is the person for you, He will let you know. Seek God's perfect will for your life, not His permissive will. Remember, what God has put together let no man, woman, family or friend put a wedge between.

His Faithful One
Lady Lorraine Foster

INTRODUCTION

This book will provide tools to empower current and future couples with helpful information toward maintaining a healthy marriage beyond the wedding day. Marriage is a sacred relationship ordained by God and should not be entered into without understanding that a marriage is much more than the wedding day.

Marriage is a partnership that exists for the betterment of both husband and wife. Marriage is a process and not an event. It would behoove couples to understand what can and will take place after the wedding day.

CONTENTS

My Context

As I begin to put pen to paper and fingers to laptop, I am reminded that some of us grew up in homes where both parents were active and present, while others grew up in homes with only one parent. It was in the latter category that I find myself. As I briefly reflect on my childhood, I realize that I felt disconnected from what I perceived as a traditional family unit. This was due in part because my father and mother divorced early into their marriage. As a result, I became the over functioning parentified child in my family of origin and lived out my childhood with the responsibilities of a "grown-up" young man. Gratefully, I learned through my mother's sacrificial love that a family is not always made up of two loving, active, and affectionate parents living under the same roof.

Unfortunately, in today's society the family structure is not what we have seen on television sitcoms like "The Cosby Show," "Fresh Prince of Bel Air," "The Bernie Mac Show," "Everybody Hates Chris," "Father Knows Best," "Leave it to Beaver" or "Little House on the Prairie." My family was not the model used by Hollywood. It was not portrayed on the big screen as the traditional, Western culture nuclear family; however, it was this family that allowed me to grow into the man of God that I am today. I want to describe what has been a productive journey for me. It has been an ongoing learning experience.

In order for you to fully appreciate who I am I need to tell you more about my contextual frame of reference. I am blessed to be the product of an African American cultural heritage that has traditionally functioned as if everyone belongs to each other. I humbly acknowledge that I am the product of those who have gone before me and I am grateful for their legacy. I am equally blessed to be the son of a preacher and come from a long line of Methodist pastors. I have a profound love for the people of God and strive to encourage all those who yield to the joy of following Jesus. I enjoy working with people and make every effort to assist them in discovering their way. According to the Myers-Briggs Type Indicator, I am categorized as an ESTJ. This is known as the Extraversion, Sensing, Thinking and Judging type. I tend to be outgoing but appreciate being by myself. My ministry has been impacted by many people. Finally, I was raised by the village and thus I will be lifting up ways in which the entire family is of value in a theology of marriage and family.

My Hermeneutical Point of Departure

My hermeneutic is greatly influenced by my understanding of the nature of the church, the person of Christ and other doctrines of my faith. The starting place for moving toward a theology of marriage and family is deeply rooted in my understanding of God's Word. "As we open our minds and hearts to the Word of God through the words of human beings inspired by the Holy Spirit, faith is born and nourished, our understanding is deepened, and the possibilities for transforming the world become apparent to us."[1] There are two basic kinds of questions that I distinguish when reading a biblical passage. They are context and content. This manner allows for proper exegesis of the text. I read and apply scripture more thoroughly when I seek to understand both the historical and literary context of a particular passage of scripture. This practice has strengthened and affirmed my understanding of God because it has allowed me to see the sovereignty and omnipresence of God.

---

1   The Book of Discipline of The United Methodist Church. (Nashville, TN: United Methodist Publishing House, 2004), p. 78.

My continued practice of ministry has further inspired me to know that God is a God of interaction. I see a relationship and a dialogue between theology and the social sciences particularly with contextual therapy. God's desire is to bring harmony to a sinful and dying world. Contextual Family therapy has similar desires. "While Nagy acknowledges no faith basis to his theory, its compatibility with Christian faith assumption and practices is evident at several important points."[2]

As I continue to be privileged to serve a risen Savior, God continues to reveal Himself through Jesus Christ's example and through the Holy Spirit. I have discovered through revelation/illumination, required readings, lectures, and my own urban ministry context, that to move toward formulating a theology of marriage and family I need to integrate my understanding of scripture and the insights gained through the models of systems theory. I choose to interact in this manner because my limited understanding of humanity is continually growing.

I believe that all God's creatures are special. Each of God's creation contains value and worth. My hermeneutic is enlightened because I find value and truth in the social sciences as well as theology. I also believe that God intended a dialogue between the two disciplines to allow for further revelation. From the very beginning, I believe God created humanity to be in relationship with one another; to be in community while at the same time being self differentiated. I believe God desires that no one be lost; that humanity would be saved through His Son Jesus Christ. The need for divine grace is always present and necessary. Divine grace is what sustains us in our journey of faith. The Bible declares that all of humanity has sinned (Romans

---

2   Manfred Brauch's PowerPoint Presentation: Contextual Therapy and Christian Faith. Palmer Theological Seminary. January 12, 2007.

3:23) and are in need of salvation. Because we can not save ourselves, we all stand in need of God's divine grace. In the giving of divine grace, I am convinced that we as humans are given a path, a doorway to travel ultimately leading to salvation. Since this is the purpose for humanity, scripture is a tool to help address this outcome. Social science on the other hand gives me additional lenses in which to see in a matter-of-fact way what theology professes on faith.

My hermeneutical point of departure is grounded and is drawn from a number of principal sources. The main sources that have helped shape my theology are: Scripture; Reason; Tradition; and Experience. I accept Scripture to be the true inspired Word of God. It is all sufficient and a primary source of my faith. "Because the Bible is God's Word, it has eternal relevance; it speaks to all humankind, in every age and in every culture."[3] The very core of my Christian witness is derived from Scripture. It is through Scripture that I understand my faith and my identity. It is because of my allegiance to Scripture that I often have a creative tension when called to integrate theology and social sciences.

Tradition is/are those things that I treasure and value as important to my faith; such as the creeds and rituals of the church. "The passing on and receiving of the gospel among persons, regions, and generations constitutes a dynamic element of Christian history."[4] Tradition provides an additional source of my understanding. My understanding is expanded by reflecting on the Patristic writings, the ecumenical creeds, the teachings of the Reformers, and the literature of contemporary spirituality.

---

3   Gordon D. Fee and Douglas Stuart. How to Read the Bible for all its Worth: A Guide to Understanding the Bible. (Grand Rapids, Michigan: Zondervan Publishing House, 1993), p. 17.

4   The Book of Discipline of The United Methodist Church. (Nashville, TN: United Methodist Publishing House, 2004) p. 79

Scripture combined with Tradition has helped to shape my theology in a more faithful way.

Experience refers to the trials, the joys and concerns I have endured. "Our experience interacts with Scripture. We read Scripture in light of the conditions and events that help shape who we are, and we interpret our experience in terms of Scripture."[5] My personal experiences have helped to demonstrate God's forgiving and empowering grace on my life. My daily reflection on the Word of God along with other secular literature and thought has allowed me to see God at work through every day situations. These experiences help me to navigate the terrain of ministry and give balance to my decisions when other disciplines are incorporated. Because of the outcome of these personal experiences, I have become wiser when making future decisions because I have a track record of the subject matter.

Reason is another element that helps shape my hermeneutic. "Although we recognize that God's revelation and our experiences of God's grace continually surpass the scope of human language and reason, we also believe that any disciplined theological work calls for the careful use of reason."[6] Reason is formulated by a way of discernment as guided by the Holy Spirit. My understanding of Scripture allows me to discern the will and the purpose of God. Reason allows me to ask critical questions of faith and causes me to seek further understanding of God's purpose. These four primary sources, each making distinctive contributions to my hermeneutic work help move me toward a theology of marriage and family. It honors the legacy of our ancestors and helps to keep me connected to those things that are meaningful and beneficial. This method has opened

---

5   Ibid., p. 81
6   Ibid., p. 82

the way for new voices to be heard, including those in the social science arena.

"There are several options for integrating social science material and theology. One view is opposition, which amounts to choosing theology over social science or social science over theology."[7] This method would cause us to choose one or the other based on the lenses or the school of thought we prefer. I believe this view causes the participant to be unaware of other sources of truth due to pre-conceived bias toward a particular discipline of study. There are a number of models of integration: Against Model, Of Model, Parallel Model, and the Integrate model. The opposition model as previously referenced is similar to the "Against" model, which is "built on the assumption that there are inherent conflicts between psychology and religion on the one hand and between Christianity and psychology on the other."[8] The correlation view and the integrative complementary view are additional ways of integration The isolationist view and the correlation view are indicative of the "Parallel" model which "maintains that psychology and the Scriptures are separate and there is little or no significant overlap (isolationist view) and the other "attempts to correlate (correlation view) or align certain psychological and scriptural concepts."[9] I choose to use the integrate model, which is more of a complementary view. The integrate model is "a model which is rooted in the assumption that God is the author of all truth. Reason, revelation and the scientific method all are seen as playing a valid role in the search for truth."[10] I choose this

---

7   Manfred Brauch's Lecture at Palmer Theological Seminary. January 12, 2007.

8   John D. Carter and Bruce Narramore. The Integration of Psychology and Theology: An Introduction. Grand Rapids, MI: Zondervan Publishing House, 1979, p. 73.

9   Ibid., 92.

10   Ibid.,p. 103.

model over the others because I believe this model is more in line with the contextual model because it gives voice to both disciplines. I believe Scripture to be authoritative and it is my primary source of revelation, however I do believe God in His sovereignty uses whatever means necessary to bring about a balanced understanding of both theology and social science. "Scripture is totally and completely sufficient regarding the establishment and maintenance of fellowship with God (salvation and sanctification), that the special revelation we have in the Bible serves as a guide for exploring general revelation; and that Scripture itself gives us precedent for how God-honoring believers used knowledge from sources other than the Bible to serve God." [11] When I am presented with a choice between theology and science, my experience combined with reason has led me to lean toward Scripture. I do recognize that there is truth in both theology and science but ultimately, I believe theology and the Holy Spirit to reveal all truth. This is my primary frame of reference when dealing with conflicts between theology and social science. Science helps us to develop a hypothesis and to prove it, while theology relates to belief and faith. A productive integration can be accomplished by seeking to hear the truth contained in both Scripture and the sciences.

My hermeneutical point of departure affirms the fact that I come to the text with limited understanding as declared by the Apostle Paul in I Corinthians 13:9, "we know only in part…" I am a finite and limited creature made in the image of God and I cannot fully understand the workings of an infinite and limitless God. For example, Anderson & Guernsey affirm that there is a

---

11   Daryl H. Stevenson, Brian E Eck, and Peter C. Psychology & Christianity Integration: Seminal Works that Shaped the Movement. Batavia, Illinois: Christian Association for Psychological Studies, Inc. 2007., p. 76.

cultural bias present in the modern interpretations of Scripture. These authors state that "whenever Scripture touches upon the nature of social roles – such as the roles of husband and wife – the interpretation of that Scripture and its application to the modern world is shaped by those assumptions."[12]   I bring to the table my own personal experience combined with traditions learned through my personal context. This is helpful when I am open to listen to both theology and the sciences. It becomes problematic when I decide to put theology over science without addressing the truth of social science. It is for this reason that I believe marriage and family must incorporate both biblical and social principles if the desire is to be productive.

I want to raise a definition that helps me to unpack my comprehension of the task of moving toward a theology of marriage and family. Disciplinary Integration "is when two or more disciplines are jointly brought to bear on the same issue so that decisions about that issue reflect the contributions of both disciplines. The issue may be about how one discipline carries out its work or may be a problem that more than one discipline work together to solve."[13]   There can be a struggle or a healthy tension when integrating two different disciplines. My center of attention on scripture causes me to wrestle with the secular tenants of social science. There will always be biases with both theology and the sciences. When those occurrences happen, I am most drawn to the authority of Scripture over social science. "This living core stands revealed in Scripture, illumined by tradition, vivified in personal and corporate experience, and

---

12   Ray S. Anderson & Dennis B. Guernsey. On Being Family: A Social Theology of the Family: (Grand Rapids, MI: Eerdmans, 1985)., p. 105.
13   Richard L. Gorsuch. Integrating Psychology and Spirituality? (Westport, Connecticut: Praegar Publishers, 2002) p. 6.

confirmed by reason."[14] It is through scripture that I encounter God's extravagant love and redeeming grace. By applying the quadrilateral to my faith, it provides a better understanding and foundation in my decision making process. It is through this theological framework I am able to handle situations of opposition as it relates to theology and the sciences. Social science however, can help emphasize the biblical mandate of forgiveness while personal experience may not excuse an abuse by a friend or family member. Negative entitlements may be explained through the sciences but does not remove the felt experience.

I have discerned through much prayer that the school of thought I will be integrating with throughout this book will be that of Contextual Family Therapy as represented by Ivan Boszormenyi-Nagy.

> "Contextual Family Therapy, developed by Ivan Boszormenyi-Nagy, focuses on relational ethics and transgenerational legacies, and how influences from the past have a bearing on present-day functioning in all members. In this view, families have invisible loyalties – obligations rooted in past generations – and unsettled accounts that must be balanced. Contextual therapy attempts to rebuild responsible, trustworthy behavior, taking into account the entitlements of all concerned. Its goal is to help dysfunctional families rebalance the give-and-take and emotional ledgers between members and develop a sense of fairness, trust, and accountability in interactions with one another."[15]

Trustworthy behavior is demonstrated when all participants act in an ethical manner. It is demonstrated when all participants are

---

14   The Book of Discipline of the United Methodist Church 2004, Nashville TN, p50, 51

15   Irene Goldenberg and Herbert Goldenberg. *Family Therapy: An Overview*, Sixth Edition (Pacific Grove, CA: Brooks/Cole Thomson, 2004) p. 211.

held accountable for their actions both past and present. Likewise, fairness among family members is present when the interests of everyone are taken into account. "Contextual therapy offers a unique approach to individuals and families. It examines complex loyalty issues across the generations in the context of the therapists' commitment to all family members, present or absent."[16]

This school of thought, as I understand it, allows the family to travel back in time to assess the patterns of behavior that caused dysfunction in the first place. It helps by giving tools to address the present dysfunction as positive entitlements and legacies. This approach gives value and voice to the entire system. The moral dimension of this type of therapy allows for accountability and fairness. I believe this approach places greater emphasis on the social and historical context of the family. I appreciate Nagy because he does not look at families in a vacuum. He sees a nuclear family as being greater than the sum of its parts. He recognizes that individual family members unconsciously bring generational issues into their decision making process by way of their behavior. I believe this method is advantageous in bringing about a sense of wholeness to the family. It gives voice to all parties and seeks justice.

I do appreciate the tenants and principles of other theorists; however, I am most drawn to Nagy. Although he is not presented as a Christian theorist, Nagy's model resembles the voice and spirit of Holy Scripture. The key concepts associated with contextual therapy such as: fairness and justice remind me of the prophet Micah when he said, "He hath shewed thee, O man, what is good; and what doth the Lord require of thee, but to do justly, and to love mercy, and to walk humbly with thy God?" (Micah 6:8)

---

16 Ofra Shaham. *Family Therapy Magazine*, September-October, 2005, pg. 34

THE CHARACTER
OF HUMANITY
(RELATIONAL DYNAMICS)

In the beginning, God created us to be in relationship with each
other. As far back as I can remember it was explained to me in
Sunday school classes that God designed us to be in relation with
each other. The creation story tells us that "God created humankind in his image, in the image of God he created them; male and
female he created them" (Genesis 1:27 NRSV). "The suggestion
here is that it is impossible to come to know the significance of our
humanity without reference to the sexual differentiation between
male and female. To be human simply is to exist in this male-
female duality."[17] "We are created not for life in isolation but for
community, a community which binds those who are different.
We are not simply "persons," however important that claim may
on occasion be as a protest against inequities."[18]

---

17   http://www.iclnet.org/pub/resources/text/wittenberg/mosynod/web/
     sxty-02.html.

18   Ibid.

Throughout history, the quest to define the nature of human persons and their character has been an ongoing process for both theologians and scientists. The sciences consistently engage in discerning what the true nature of human beings is. Its conventional methods help to define the nature of humanity. "All relationship systems are conservative. Their logic demands that the members' shared investment of care and concern should serve to balance out all injustices and exploitations."[19] A conservative system believes in established institutions and natural law.

Contextual therapy language such as: fairness, justice, ledgers, legacy, loyalty splits, and multilateral partiality give support to the understanding of relational dynamics. Contextual therapy assists in providing a healthy balanced ledger. It facilitates dialogue and direct exchanges that lead to positive entitlement within relationships. Relational ethics focuses attention on the long-term, oscillating balance of equality among members within a family. This is accomplished by giving proper value to each person in the system.

"Contrary to the myth of self-sufficiency, the human being was made for companionship. Our dependence on relationships with other people is one of the most obvious facts about us. We are drawn to other people and them to us."[20] A person cannot exist by themselves. We are social beings designed to live in community.

In meeting our own needs, we must keep in mind the needs of others because this is the divine intent for our very existence.

---

19   Ivan Boszormenyi-Nagy & Geraldine M. Spark. *Invisible Loyalties: Reciprocity in Integenerational Family Therapy.* (New York: Bruner/ Mazel Publishers, 1984), p. 11.

20   David P. Gushee. *Getting Marriage Right: Realistic Counsel for Saving & Strengthening Relationships.* (Baker Books: Grand Rapids MI, 2004), p. 94.

"As noted, two individuals relating together are not independent; they mutually influence one another."[21] This designed purpose is tainted with the reality that we often miss the mark. This is due to our choice to engage in activity that is contrary to the will of God. Social science would view this as a dysfunction. Contextual theorists and theology would agree that we are social beings created for community. The negative choices we make affect people at different levels of their relationship. There is no such thing as private sin; the sins of one person affect others directly or indirectly.

We are interconnected and should make choices that will honor God, and humanity. When we are obedient, we strengthen our relationships and minimize the dysfunction that follows disobedience. How we interact with each other helps to define who we are in relationship to each other. Ivan Boszormenyi-Nagy focuses on the systemic realities of human relatedness. Contextual therapy describes the transactional patterns that are embedded in the family as a system. These transactional patterns are not always obvious. They also may not be readily accepted. Our ability to relate to one another is directly linked to our sense of fairness and justice. If we are hurt or abused as a child, the psychological impact of that event can be carried into adulthood. If the experience is not acknowledged or dealt with, the result can be transacted from one generation to another. Family members or spouses can have that event projected onto them without their knowledge. Fairness and justice are the result when both parties make amends or when one party is exonerated from their injury.

We can spend a lifetime trying to discover who we are. It

---

21   Dorothy Stroh Becvar & Raphael J. Becvar. *Family Therapy: A Systemic Integration* (Pearson Education: Needham Heights, MA, 2000), pg. 75.

is clear however, that we cannot fully know who we are without the feedback and input of others. "It requires work to be and become a person. Much of the work is our own; part of it belongs to others who are related to us in some way."[22] It is through our understanding of ourselves that we really become relational. The nature of human relatedness, primarily as expressed in marriage and family, is understood and viewed through the lenses of scripture and social science. We were all made in the image of God, fearfully and wonderfully made. "Although Christians have forgotten it, our bodily limits including our maleness and femaleness were given to us as the media in which to develop the gift of God's image."[23] Humanity is at its best when there is an acknowledgement that it is in a relational structure that affirms the unique differences of male and female. This is affirmed in Scripture as mentioned in the covenant relationship between man and woman in the context of marriage as found in Gen. 2:18-25 and Mark 10:6-9. The basic structure of human identity and existence is relatedness or community. It is through community that we become as God purposed whether married or single. God is no respecter of person and neither does he frown upon his creation if they desire to remain single. "Not every human being need enter the order of marriage (1 Cor. 7:1-7). Celibacy is also in accordance with the will of God. Despite the justifiable polemic of the Reformers against the view of medieval Christendom which institutionalized celibacy as a way of life more acceptable to God than the marital union of husband and wife, we cannot allow that

---

22 G. Peter Schreck's handout entitled: *Personhood and Relational Life Tasks: A Model for Integrating Psychology and Theology.* January 2007 Intensive, Palmer Theological Seminary, p. 78.

23 Mary Stewart Van Leeuwen. *Gender & Grace: Love, Work & Parenting in a Changing World.* (Downers Grove, Illinois, InterVarsity Press, 1990), p. 76

polemic to determine everything we say about the fellowship of man and woman."[24]

"The male-female union of marriage and its fruit-bearing – as a fulfillment of the command "be fruitful and multiply" – is likely not the intention/will of God for each particular human being or each particular marriage"[25] "Throughout the biblical story, there are examples of divinely affirmed singleness. Indeed, Paul argues for its preference in various situations on the basis of historical, theological, or missiological grounds as recorded in I Corinthians 7. The incarnate life of Christ – as the "new Adam" is a full expression of the divine image within the context of human (creaturely) limitation as reflected in II Corinthians 4:4; Col 1:15, 19; 2:9. This is potent affirmation that the relationship of marriage is not in any way a superior relational expression of the "image of God"[26] Both married and single persons are part of the body of Christ and therefore, neither are more important than the other because they both reflect the image of God. "And we recognize that some that do not choose the single state may, nevertheless, live such a life. They too exist within the duality of male and female. They too live as male and female. The Christian community needs to be sensitive to the needs of all single persons in its midst, including those who for various reasons are unable to marry or who may have lost their spouse through death or divorce."[27]

Our view on our sexuality helps to define who we are in our relationships whether single or married. "Sexual intercourse is

24 http://www.iclnet.org/pub/resources/text/wittenberg/mosynod/web/sxty-02.html.

25 Manfred Brauch's Lecture *at Palmer Theological Seminary.* January 12, 2007

26 Ibid.

27 http://www.iclnet.org/pub/resources/text/wittenberg/mosynod/web/sxty-02.html.

carefully placed within the context of marriage throughout the Scriptures. This idea is so strong that unmarried persons who engage in intercourse are regarded as entering into a one-flesh union similar to marriage."[28] "God created humans with the capacity for intimate, passionate sex throughout their married life."[29] I believe that we have the responsibility to be accountable in our relationships especially in our sexual encounters as they are a reflection of our understanding of God. I also believe that when this is done, we are operating in what contextual therapy describes as "an ethical guarantee" or an entitlement within the relationship. "Authentic sexual expression based on covenant, grace and empowering principles is most likely to occur in long-term committed relationships."[30] I would contend that the same thought is present in the minds of single persons based on research indicating an increase in pre-marital sex. Because God created us as sexual beings, we must live out that reality in ways that honor our creator. "Authentic sexuality, then, brings authenticity to ourselves and our relationships as it reflects God's divine intention for who are and how we are to behave as sexual relational beings."[31]

---

28 Judith K. Balswick & Jack O. Balswick. *Authentic Human Sexuality: An Integrated Christian Approach.* Downers Grove, IL: Intervarsity Press, 1999., p. 111.

29 Ibid., p. 150.

30 Ibid., p. 150.

31 Ibid., p. 36.

HUMAN DEVELOPMENT

"*Psychology recognizes that human beings* are historical creatures in that our past lives on and influences the present
and the future."[32] The persons that we are today are a culmination
of the past lessons learned and the experiences embraced. Our
past experiences for good or for bad help to shape our human
development. It is through our human relationships that our
development is strengthened. "Eric Erickson maintained that we
develop according to a ground plan and that what we achieve or
fail to achieve, in childhood becomes the foundation on which we
build later in life."[33] Our human development can be hindered
if we do not recognize the significance of our past experiences.
Contextual therapy also recognizes that our human development
is historical by placing others in an intergenerational context.

Other social scientists including Sigmund Freud assert that
we are biological beings, but as a Christian, I believe we are more
than just a body. Our human development is a compilation of

---

32 Leroy Aden, David G. Benner, & J. Harold Ellens. *Christian
Perspectives on Human Development.* (Michigan: Baker Book House
Publishing, 1992), p. 11.
33 Ibid, p. 11.

both biological and social interaction. The bible speaks of development as it relates to the spiritual maturity of believers. The example as referenced in Hebrews 5:12-14 of moving from milk to meat in some ways reminds me of human development. Human development is not based on our chronological age as alluded to in scripture; rather it is obtained at different levels of our developmental journey.

There are several basic human psychological needs that are directly associated with the eight stages of Christian growth and human development. According to Captain, the stages are as follows: Innocence (1) Nurturance (2), Obedience (3), Behavior (4), Motive (5), Meaning (6), Love (7), and Fruit Stage (8). "Our first psychospiritual stage of human development is the Innocence Stage. This stage involves the baby in the womb of the mother and runs from conception to birth."[34] "The basic human need for the Nurturance Stage is security. This stage covers the period from birth to the age of two. The need for security is defined here as the state the infant experiences when his or her needs are adequately met."[35] The Obedience Stage takes place outside of the mother's womb. This stage covers the period of age two to the age of six. "Within the child's drive for autonomy and self-exploration, the child has no concept of danger. As a result, without the protection of limits established by a loving authority figure, the child will eventually hurt him/herself."[36] In this stage, a child is given some liberty and loving authority to bring about a healthy balance. The Behavior Stage shifts from liberty to discerning right from wrong. This stage covers the period of six to twelve years of age. The

---

34 Philip A. Captain. *Eight Stages of Christian Growth: Human Development in Psycho-Spiritual Terms.* (New Jersey: Prentice-Hall, Inc., 1984), p. 31.

35 Ibid., p. 14.

36 Ibid., p. 14.

emphasis during this period is on learning and skill development. The primary need for this stage is competency. "The need for competency is based on the idea that all children need to feel they are a success."[37] The next stage is the Motive Stage. This covers the adolescent years from approximately age twelve to the age of twenty. "In this stage, focus must shift from the child's behavior to the child's inner self – the mind and the heart. This stage is a time of confusion as the adolescent begins to try to understand his or her own thoughts, feelings, and motives."[38] The next stage is the Meaning Stage of young adulthood. This stage covers the period of age twenty to age thirty. "In this stage the young adult must find commitment. Each young adult must find a cause in which to believe. It is through this cause that life takes on purpose."[39] The next stage of development is the Love stage. This stage covers the periods of age twenty-five to forty-five. "The Love Stage centers on marriage and the family unit, although adult friendships can also be quite important to many people. The emphasis changes from one's role in life to one's relationships with people."[40] Intimacy is important to this stage as this stage allows for the development of relationships. The final stage is the Fruit stage. This stage covers the periods of age forty and beyond. "This stage begins at a point in life when people begin to spend more time looking back and reminiscing than looking forward and planning."[41] In this stage, the primary need is value and significance.

There are other thoughts on human development that are similar and are confirmed by other authors. There are four major theories of development according to Neil J. Salkind.

---

37   Ibid., p. 15.
38   Ibid., p. 16.
39   Ibid., p. 16.
40   Ibid., p. 17.
41   Ibid., p. 18.

They are: "Maturational, Psychoanalytic, Behavioral, and Organismic. Maturational theory assumes the sequence of development is determined by biological factors. Psychoanalytic theory assumes development consists of dynamic, structural, and sequential components. Behavioral theory assumes development occurs according to the laws of learning and places great importance in the environment. Organismic theory assumes development consists of the addition and modification of psychological structures."[42]

The maturational model believes human development is determined by the natural and evolutionary history of the species. In other words, human development is primarily under the control of biological systems and the process of maturing through internal stimuli. Conversely, the behavioral model places most of its emphasis on human development through external stimuli in the environment. "For example, if one is interested in studying an aspect of mother-infant interaction, behaviors are explicitly defined and must be objective enough to be reliably measured. Such constructs as "nice feelings" would not meet such criteria, but "number of times mother touches infant" would."[43] The organismic model of development places emphasis on the individual's active role rather than a reactive role. The transition between different stages of development is essential in this model of maturity. The psychoanalytic model of development "consists of dynamic, structural, and sequential components, each influenced by a continuously renewed need for the gratification of basic instincts."[44]

These developmental stages occur in all human beings

---

42 Neil J. Salkind. *Theories of Human Development*. (New York: Litton Educational Publishing. 1981), p. 12.

43 Ibid., p. 17.

44 Ibid., 15.

regardless of where they reside on the globe. "Generativity is primarily the interest in establishing and guiding the next generation, although there are people who, from misfortune or because of special and genuine gifts in other directions, do not apply this drive to offspring."[45]

When I was a child, I was told that much of who we are is greatly determined by the environment in which we are raised, be it urban, suburban, or rural. My theology of marriage and family as it relates to my identity is fully in line with the redemptive and restorative efforts of the Gospel. I am comforted in the fact that although I am greatly influenced by my family of origin, I do not have to remain stuck in their frame of reference. For example, my understanding of Ezekiel 18:17-22, as it relates to generational curses, has allowed me to develop more wisdom in the area of my physical health. The intergenerational patterns inherited in human development can be better transacted when informed decisions are made. The dialogue between my faith and the sciences has allowed me to trust more in God than the environment which I was raised. I believe my human development would be diminished if I chose to be hindered by what has happened in my family over several generations. It is through this systemic framework that we find the nature of our personhood. Our basic faith, our initial connection to God and the universe comes from what James Fowler defines as Primal Faith. He states that primal faith begins as a "predisposition of trust and loyalty toward the environment into which we emerge."[46]

Our purpose as human beings is realized when we understand

---

45 Erik H. Erickson. *Identity and the Life Cycle.* (New York: W.W. Norton & Company, 1980), p. 103.

46 James W. Fowler. *Becoming Adult, Becoming Christian: Adult Development & Christian Faith.* (San Francisco, Ca.: Jossey-Bass Publishers, 2000) pg. 58.

that our faith in God and our understanding of the social sciences will give us the tools that will bring about a healthy integration. Scripture admonishes us in Ephesians 6:13-17, to put on the whole armor of God. Just as this passage breaks down the pieces of armor that we are to wear, our human development needs to be broken down into digestible parts. It is when we understand and accomplish the tasks associated with the different stages or parts that we are able to fully mature as relational beings.

The Personality
of the Family
(Relational Ethics)

Imagine with me what I believe a healthy family looks like, or at best should strive to be. A healthy family provides an atmosphere of warmth, tenderness, and safety. In this proposed paradigm, secrets are few, if they exist at all. No subject matter is off-limits including religion and politics. These homes are warm, and the communication is open and consistent. Children know they are loved and valued in a healthy family. The parents seek out their opinions and care about their well being. The parents in a healthy family do not view the children as "small adults" who can fend for themselves. Rather they receive them as gifts, blessings that need nurturance. They are trained in a manner that promotes their growth into healthy adults who in turn raise healthy children. The children are not obligated to be seen and not heard. They are encouraged to make noise while having fun which is only natural and expected. They are permitted to have friends over because good parents recognize this as a way of developing their social skills. In this type of family the children interact with their parents easily. The family members are sensitive to one another. They express their caring with an occasional touch, a hug or with questions that help them to understand each other more clearly. Meal time in this family is a time when everyone is expected to be at the table to enjoy being family.

What I have attempted to describe may sound like a fantasy family, but I believe if we are intentional in our quest to create a healthy family, every effort must be employed, even if it seems far-fetched. I thought it might be helpful if I included in this book a definition of family. "The family is a group of persons with a past history, a present reality, and a future expectation of interconnected trans-generational relationships. Members often (but not necessarily) are bound together by heredity, by legal marital ties, by adoption, or by a common living arrangement at some point in their lifetime."[47] "Today the family in our society is certainly far from healthy. The only question seems to be: How sick is it; Unto death, or only badly ailing?"[48]

I believe that unmet expectations can lead to disappointment and possibly separation and divorce. The moral principles needed to sustain any family must be more than the overt and covert expectations placed on the family. It has been said, "To whom much is given, from him much will be required" (Luke 12:48). Families have been given one of the greatest gifts, the gift of each other. In receiving that gift, more than mere words must be demonstrated in the general maintenance of the family, especially in the area of relational ethics. Relational ethics is, "a

47 Jeannette R. Kramer. *Family Interfaces: Transgenerational Patterns.* (New York: Brunner/Mazel Publishers, 1985), p.3.

48 Manfred Brauch's handout entitled: *Issues of Biblical Authority and a Theology of The Family. Palmer Theological Seminary.* January 12, 2007, p. 2.

chain of interlocking consequences in relationships between the generations. One's behavior is rooted in the past and, at the same time, will affect future generations."[49]

Families, like marriages, are organisms. It is a delicate and at times a fragile entity that needs to have a great amount of intentional time dedicated to it in order for it to grow and flourish. Marriage requires work. There needs to be an intentional plan to ensure its success. Thus the male-female coming together in marriage and its fruit-bearing – as a realization of the command "be fruitful and multiply" – is probably not the intention of God for each particular human being or each particular marriage. All marriages do not produce children, but all marriages can grow to be productive in their relationship building.

It is my conviction that an open dialogue between theology and the social sciences will affirm the need for all people to be valued. This conversation happens when the truth of both disciplines are valued.

It is equally clear that humanity does not always operate in the perfect will of God. It is through our failure to be obedient that we bring dysfunction within our families and marriages. "When relationships are not balanced, people become disengaged from caring for others and being accountable to them (as well as to self). This leads to destructive entitlement – vengeful or spiteful behaviors by the entitled one."[50] In every area of our lives there is always the possibility of incurring unavoidable and sometimes unwanted situations. The nature of brokenness in marriage is not exempt from this reality. Just as a marriage is seen as a living organism, we must also recognize the toxic nature of humanity.

---

rna L. Hecker, Joseph L. Wetchler. *An Introduction to Marriage and nily Therapy.* (New York: Hayworth Press Inc., 2003), p. 290.
., p. 275.

Unexpected threat in the marriage are inevitable by the mere fact that husband and wife, man and woman, come into the marriage from different places, possibly spiritually, definitely physically. In acknowledging the uniqueness and individuality of each other through validation, the marriage will be able to better handle the toxic matters that occur in the marriage covenant. These differences are present when husband and wife are able to be themselves in the midst of being a couple. Differences are present when husband and wife respect the differences of their unique backgrounds. I am convinced that when we are really genuine with ourselves and with God then reconciliation is the possibility and the promise that is ours.

Additionally, risks have more teeth and power, when we allow ourselves to become "indifferent," in other words, when we take on a "don't care" attitude. The possibility of peace (shalom-wholeness) is more readily received when husband and wife care enough about each other to "fight the good fight," in love and because of the love of God, we are able to be restored by God.

INVISIBLE LOYALTIES

The best way for me to describe my understanding of Invisible Loyalties is to acknowledge the fact that I was and in some ways still am a parentified child. "By definition, parentification implies the subjective distortion of a relationship as if one's partner or even children were his parent."[51] "Parentification is an expectation within a family system, and its target is chosen according to complex determinants. For instance, it usually is not one parent who elects the scapegoat but the family system as a whole."[52] Invisible loyalties can cause alignments, splits and alliances within both the family of origin and procreation. These elements have a way of changing the fabric of families for generations to come, sometimes in subtle yet life altering ways. "Between the continuously succeeding generations are imbedded the vertical bonds of loyalty: the asymmetrical, irreversible relationship between parents and child."[53] Invisible loyalties are present in families and

---

51 Ibid., p. 151.
52 Ibid., p. 161.
53 Ammy van Heusden, ElseMarie van den Eerenbeemt. *Balance in Motion: Ivan Boszormenyi-Nagy and His Vision of Individual and Family Therapy.* (New York: Brunner/Mazel Publishers, 1987), p. 19.

marriages. "If the act of falling in love is always partly based in imaginary parentification, then most marriages can be considered as subsequent life-long contracts for balancing this fantasy with responsible and giving marital mutuality."[54] This can prove to be difficult in the marriage when the parentified child must choose the level of and loyalty to the family of origin. "The patterns of parentification in families illustrate how obligations operate in shaping relationships among members."[55]

"The concept of loyalty can be defined in moral, philosophical, political, and psychological terms. Conventionally, it has been described as a reliable, positive, attitude of individuals toward what has been called the "object" of loyalty."[56] "The origins of loyalty commitments are typically dialectical in nature. Their internalized pattern originates from something owed to a parent or to an internalized image of a parent representative (superego)."[57] "We assume that in order to be a loyal member of a group, one has to internalize the spirit of its expectations and to have a set of specifiable attitudes to comply with the internalized injunctions. Ultimately, the individual can thus be subjected to the injunctions of both external expectations and internalized obligations."[58]

Scripture admonishes us to "honor our mother and father, so that our days may be long upon the earth" (Matthew 15:4). This command can bring about unforeseen or unwanted events within a marriage or family. This is what Nagy refers to as Invisible Loyalties. Invisible loyalties can be problematic to a marriage in

---

54 Ivan Boszormenyi-Nagy & Geraldine M. Spark. *Invisible Loyalties: Reciprocity in Integenerational Family Therapy.* (New York: Bruner/Mazel Publishers, 1984), p. 151.
55 Ibid., p. 163.
56 Ibid.,p 37.
57 Ibid., p.46.
58 Ibid., p.37.

that, "the loyalty system point of view implies that commitment to one's spouse may be secondary to an implicit indebtedness to yet-born offspring."[59]   Invisible loyalties are present when, "the adult is eager to impart his own normative value orientation to his child; he now becomes the "creditor" in a dialogue of commitments, in which the child becomes the "debtor."[60] The debt is repaid in the form of invisible loyalties to the creditor by living out or up to the implied or explicit expectations.

Loyalty can be defined as having an allegiance to someone or something. It usually involves a commitment to the object of your loyalty. Parents can consciously and unconsciously demand a sense of entitlement from their children. This can be done in subtle but psychological damaging ways. "Our interest in loyalty as both a group characteristic and a personal attitude surpasses the simple behavioral notion of law-abiding behavior."[61] A child can be asked to do something unhealthy or even dangerous, however, the child does so without regard for their safety because they feel a sense of "honoring their mother and father" by completing the task. Acts such as this can lead to depression and other disorders. Loyalties are also generational. They are both vertical and horizontal. "Vertical loyalty commitments are owed to either a previous or subsequent generation; horizontal loyalty commitments are owed to one's mate, siblings, or peers in general."[62] For instance, my marriage experienced vertical loyalty when my father was lying on his death bed and instructed me to care for his mother upon his death. This created a tension with

---

59   Ivan Boszormenyi-Nagy & Geraldine M. Spark. *Invisible Loyalties: Reciprocity in Integenerational Family Therapy.* (New York: Bruner/Mazel Publishers, 1984), p .48.

60   Ibid., p. 47.

61   Ibid., p. 37.

62   Ibid., p. 51.

my horizontal commitment to my wife and family of procreation. It also produced an environment that had three generations living under the same roof. The emotional and physical adjustments took a toll on my household.

Entitlements are another form of loyalty, both overt and covert. Entitlements are payments due to an individual by virtue of the fact that they are born or give birth, plus any merit that they earn. If a debt is not able to be paid back, it creates an unbalanced or unfair ledger of entitlement. "Loyalty to the family can be considered a competitive choice when outside involvements are considered. The question of preferential commitment becomes more important. The more the scope of significant relationships is limited."[63] Invisible loyalties can be understood as the inability to discern what is present, even if this is evident to others. Invisible loyalties can create many challenges and potential problems within the family. They may lead to various dysfunctions including separation, divorce, and mental anguish. In seeking advice from your parents because this was the pattern in your family of origin can be a potential to create dysfunction in your marriage and thus is and can be an example of an invisible loyalty. Keeping a standing holiday dinner commitment such as Thanksgiving or Christmas gathering with your family of origin can also be seen as an invisible loyalty. Invisible loyalties are not always negative. They have the potential to develop an awareness of future situations in the relationship.

Because marriage is a product of more than one family; more than one set of personalities, it stands to reason that there can and most often will be some degree of influence asserted by one or both families of origin. This degree of influence can manifest itself in an overt or covert manner. Nagy states that "we must

---

63 Ibid., p. 161.

consider the deepest human understructure if relationships are to consist of a network (hierarchy) of obligations."[64]

It is because of invisible loyalties that families are overloading its members with excessive commitment and responsibilities. "This overloading is probably connected with a diminishing commitment to the extended family, religion, and nationalism, and also related to a generalized feeling of alienation in modern man."[65] These expectations can be written or implied rules followed by the family members. It can be as simple as continuing a family tradition of coming together to celebrate anniversaries or birthdays. This can prove to be a problem, especially if there is great physical distance. It becomes problematic when the family of origin expects the family of procreation to comply with past events especially in blended families. These expectations can be present even before you think about creating a family of procreation. Bailing a family member out of financial distress can be an invisible loyalty. Making excuses for an unwise sibling or parent can be an invisible loyalty. These invisible loyalties, if not understood can lead to a false sense of duty, fairness and justice within the family structure. Persons within the family are often led down a path of indebtedness and ultimately a place of guilt. "Loyalty commitments are like invisible but strong fibers which hold together complex pieces of relationship "behavior" in families as well as in larger society."[66]

Theology would affirm that our actions are a by product of our relationships as the following would suggest: The biblical account of Esau and Jacob (Genesis 25:19-34) furthers supports

---

64 Ivan Boszormenyi-Nagy & Geraldine M. Spark. *Invisible Loyalties: Reciprocity in Integenerational Family Therapy.* (New York: Bruner/Mazel Publishers, 1984), p. 19.

65 Ibid., p. 162.

66 Ibid., p. 39.

the struggles faced in rearing our children from inception (two nations in the same womb). These two boys practiced in the womb what they would experience out of the womb. The jostling and crushing inside their mother would later cause physical and emotional pain to the family. Even though Esau and Jacob were twins (fraternal) their personalities were not similar. In addition to their personality differences, another element was added to the mix. Isaac and Rebekah added fuel to the sibling rivalry by choosing one son over the other (Isaac-Esau; Rebekah-Jacob). By means of deceptive scheming set up by Rebekah, Jacob managed to get Esau's blessing from the nearly blind Isaac.

Another popular narrative worth mentioning is about Joseph the dreamer (Genesis 37:1-50:26). This biblical record gives an account of Jacob's family; his love for Joseph and Joseph's dreams; the sale of Joseph into bondage; the brother's concealing the sale of Joseph from Jacob, and the selling of Joseph to Potiphar. The saga begins with the deep love for Rachel's first born. Jacob gives Joseph the symbol of his favor in a richly ornamented robe or cloak. Likewise, God favors Joseph with two dreams. The interpretation of these dreams angered Joseph's brothers and led them to stripping off his robe (his favored position) and throwing him into a pit, subsequently selling him to a caravan of Ishmaelites coming from Gilead. The theme of this narrative is retribution or vengeance. I believe the invisible loyalties expressed in these biblical stories are indicative of the retribution or vengeance often experienced by our families.

I believe the closer the relationship; the more influence or invisible loyalty is present. If a family desires to be strong and vibrant, all concerned must realize that there will be incidents that will "test the waters" of their familial commitments and at the same time present some challenging and tough decisions on behalf of the family of procreation. Insight and understanding of invisible loyalties can be an asset to the family. It can be a source of valuable information in discerning what measures are needed to bring about a healthy resolution. It can also be helpful in moving from forgiveness to exoneration which allows for a new framework to balance the ledger created by legacies.

THE NATURE OF MARRIAGES (INTENTIONALITY)

The American Heritage Dictionary defines intentionality as "the property of being about or directed toward a subject, as inherent in conscious states, beliefs, or creations of the mind, such as sentences or books." I believe marriages must be intentional or deliberate if they are to be productive. Steps must be taken to bring about harmony in the relationship.

I remember watching a television commercial in which two elderly persons are walking along a winding path in a tree lined area. Each held the hand of the beloved and cherished the company of each other's presence. I assumed the couple was husband and wife but the commercial did not state that fact. I further assumed that they had been married for a long time because of their well-groomed gray hair neatly tucked beneath their hats. They seemed to be deeply in love with each other as they strolled along the path.

Throughout Scripture we read about many different relationships. Some of them are good and some are not so good. I don't believe anyone can attain a perfect relationship or marriage, but it should not prevent us from trying. Not all marriages are made in heaven nor are they all Christian. When two non-Christians marry or when a Christian and a non-Christian marry, they are really setting themselves up for a lot of heartache. The Bible declares that marriages should not be unevenly yoked. 2 Cor. 6:14 (KJV) Be ye not unequally yoked together with unbelievers: for what fellowship hath righteousness with unrighteousness? and what communion hath light with darkness? God will indeed bless the faithfulness of his children. As soon at this choice is made, it is by no means a heavenly union. It can prove to be hell on earth. Ungodliness always brings about sorrow, sadness and damnation to your soul. It brings about the judgment warranted by the deed. Hosea 8:7 reminds us that "sown the wind and they shall reap the whirlwind." In other words, when we sow unfruitful seeds, those seeds that are not in alignment with the Word of God, we eventually will reap what we have sown.

Intentional marriages, marriages that are not entered into lightly, but advisedly, are marriages of the heart. I believe that marriages must have a strong sense of intentionality in keeping their wedding vows. The intentionality to be faithful, authentic and loving must be communicated in different ways. If they are committed to their wedding vows, I would think they would commit themselves to create a vibrant and healthy relationship. Couples do not lessen in their personhood or value when they grow in the way that God has intended for them.

Marriages should have three essential components to ensure success: communication, communication, communication. Healthy marriages don't just happen. They are not obtained by waving a magic wand. Healthy marriages require a concerted effort to communicate. It requires a willingness to be vulnerable and transparent. Marriages are sealed and held together by the intentionality of husband and wife. Love is at the heart of marriage as it is at the heart of God. Love, however, is not enough to sustain a marriage. There are other ingredients needed to keep a marriage healthy. In addition to love, there should be freedom and responsibility. When two people are able to disagree they are free to love. When they are not free, they live in fear and ultimately their love dies. I John 4:18 reminds us that "perfect love drives out fear." When two people take on the responsibility to do what is necessary to make their marriage work, love tends to grow. Conversely, if only one person takes on the bulk of the relationship, resentment can build up and the consequences are usually not pleasant for all concerned. Marriages must develop a deliberate strategy to keep the covenant intact. This requires intentionality from both husband and wife.

Too many couples engage in a matrimonial mess primarily because they do not enter the marriage with a mind-set that says "to death do we part"; in other words they often enter the marriage covenant with a sense of "if I don't like it, I'll just get out." This reminds me of a game we used to play when I was a child. The game was called king ball or four squares. Occasionally while serving the ball, it would go outside of the playing area and we would insistently demand a "do over." This was a simple and quick way to a new start and hopefully a better one. Unfortunately, marriage is not a game. Marriage at its best should be a thriving and growing organism. It should be an entity that desires to flourish and mature. This is done by keeping the marriage covenant to be faithful unto death or forever, whichever comes first.

The permanence of marriage is one of the hallmarks and bedrock of the Christian faith. Any activity outside the marriage covenant to include adultery, promiscuity and the like would result in a distortion and misrepresentation of the divinely ordered plan of God. God's plan was and is to bring about unity in the body, specifically unity between husband and wife. "The expressions of "bone of my bone" and "flesh of my flesh" as contained in Genesis 2:23-25 are "signs of exclusive, permanent "belonging". [67] Permanence in the marriage has in it the reality that God makes and keeps the promises God has made. In this idea and design of permanence, it should also be understood that the husband and wife should strive on a daily basis to honor the covenant made. In this understanding, I believe that in our faithfulness to the covenant, God in effect gives us tools to have a healthy union. The future is secured because the promises are honored. Contextual therapy emphasizes the ethical or justice dimension of close relationships. It looks at the role of caring, particularly in the area of loyalty, guilt, fairness, accountability, and trustworthiness. Permanence in the marriage can be obtained when the aforementioned elements of contextual therapy are realized.

In further solidifying the marriage covenant, it must also be understood that the husband and wife must be willing and able to strive to forgive bilaterally and not unilaterally. In doing this, it allows for both to be vulnerable to each other and be there for each other. It allows for a deeper connection within the marriage context by allowing a more intimate and personal view of the biblical understanding of husband and wife. It also reminds the couple of the fulfillment of God's irrevocable connection to Israel; the bride fully adorned for her husband. Any activity outside the marriage covenant would result in a distortion and misrepresentation of the divinely ordered plan. God's plan was

---

67   Manfred Brauch's handout entitled: *The Biblical Ideal of Exclusiveness and Permanence in the Male-Female relation of Marriage. Palmer Theological Seminary.* January 12, 2007

and is to bring about unity in the body, specifically unity between husband and wife.

Conversely, the outcome of marriage can be reversed or disconnected if we allow external and internal agents to enter into the marriage covenant. Imagine a well crafted tailor made tapestry that will be displayed in your favorite room. This tapestry was conceived and crafted in a manner that would withstand the elements and the strain of age. Now imagine that same work of art experiencing rips and tears in the very fiber and fabric that holds it together. This is what happens when married couples allow or fall prey or succumb to temptations that lead to infidelity and indiscretion within the marriage covenant. Marriage is designed to be a lasting and permanent institution. When husbands and wives begin to submit, or complement and support one another out of respect and reverence to God, the temptations that present themselves are tempered by the faithfulness of a loving and almighty God. His desire is to maintain the marriage covenant. If marriages would emulate Jesus' example of submitting to the heavenly Father out of love then our actions would demonstrate love toward each other in the marriage context. Permanence in the marriage has in it the reality that God makes and keeps the promises he has made.

What does God say about divorce? Scripture records in the gospel of Matthew19:8 the following: "He said to them, 'Moses, because of the hardness of your hearts, permitted you to divorce your wives, but from the beginning it was not so.'" Additionally, Matthew 19:8 states, "And I say to you, whoever divorces his wife, except for sexual immorality, and marries another, commits adultery and whoever marries her who is divorced commits adultery." A person could interpret this passage to suit their own preconceived ideas about divorce. They can pull out what they wanted to justify the dismantling of the marriage. I believe the biblical record speaks for itself when Jesus is clearly saying divorce is wrong. From the very beginning, God ordained marriage and it was humanity who corrupted marriage with adultery and all sorts of perversion which prompted the need for divorce. "Although the principle of earning entitlement through offering due consideration implies a built-in internal reward for the giver, this does not imply that self-sacrifice has to be viewed as destructive."[68] I believe marriages end in divorce when the partners consistently feel they are not benefiting from the marriage. Feelings of physical and emotional abandonment, unfaithfulness and abuse are additional factors that lead to the dissolve of a marriage.

My Methodist lenses (scripture, tradition, reason and experience) have taught me to discover that the law against divorce was given for three reasons. The first was to protect the family as referenced in Mark 10:6-9; secondly, to protect the land or nation preventing national disintegration as referenced in Matthew 19:1-12, Ephesians 5:22-23 and 1 Cor. 7:12-16; and finally to prevent someone from becoming an adulterer as recorded in Matthew 19:19, "I tell you that anyone who divorces his wife, except for marital unfaithfulness, and marries another woman commits adultery."

The biblical exception for divorce is the sin of marital unfaithfulness being committed by one of the spouses. The great tragedy of sexual immorality or adultery is that it breaks the union and attachment between husband and wife and ultimately destroys families for years to come. The intergenerational effects of divorce can be life altering. The children of divorced parents are often left to decide who to align with.

---

68 Journal of Marital and Family Therapy, April 1997, pg. 173.

COMPLEMENTARITY

*M*arriage of reciprocated empowerment doesn't come naturally or without human intention. The tendency in marriage is to dominate in order to guarantee personal interests. I believe that one of the central issues that create a division and a barrier between marital equality is the authority issue. Much of the argument or the controversy can usually be around the language we use to describe marital roles and responsibilities. Most would agree that marriage is a partnership, but some define partnership and its application in many different ways. There are many different ways of promoting harmony and peace within the context of marriage and family. One way is to acknowledge each others worth in the marriage. Another way is to create opportunities for positive reinforcement. If a person takes into account his own interests as well as the interests of the other and in that way establishes equilibrium of mutual interests, he earns merit and is entitled to the acknowledgement of the other."[69] These opportunities can be obtained by being flexible and adaptable

---

69   Ammy van Heusden, ElseMarie van den Eerenbeemt. *Balance in Motion: Ivan Boszormenyi-Nagy and His Vision of Individual and Family Therapy.* (New York: Brunner/Mazel Publishers, 1987), p. 43.

to life circumstances; allowing for input on setting and keeping priorities; focusing on the essentials, and drawing on all the resources available to help meet the demands of family life. It may become necessary to accommodate the individual strengths of each partner. For example, one spouse may pull back from work commitments in order to give more time to family life at a particular family stage. Then at another time, the other spouse makes adjustments by taking on more childcare and decreasing employment responsibilities. These acts will lead to more nurturing of the marriage in a way that honors each other's commitments. The scenery and the environment of the family must be understood if it is to be as God ordained in its fullest context. The family must be seen as a work in progress. It is an organism that needs the input of all concerned.

In developing a theology of marriage and family as it relates to nurture, the most optimum place to start in my opinion is by adopting and utilizing the example and pattern given to us by Jesus' life which was intentionally demonstrated through the event of his life a pattern for all interpersonal relationships, including marriages and families. Jesus lived out the true meaning of looking after and caring for the family in ways that usually was contradictory to contemporary society's understanding of leadership. In seeking a true understanding of nurture, a genuine and intentional approach must be employed. The following passages of Scripture are blueprints that will help to provide an accurate scope for which to develop a context for nurturing in the context of marriage and family: Mark 8:31-38; Mark 9:30-37; Mark 10:32-45; Luke 22:24-27; John 13; Philippians 2:5-11. In each of the aforementioned passages, Jesus gives us the example and the direction in which proper stewardship must be employed if we are to have an authentic and beneficial framework for nurturing the marriage and the family in a Christian context. "To be created male and female means that in the equality of personhood there is a complementarity of service within the framework of love (agape)."[70]

A marriage can only be as strong as its weakest member, recognizing neither person is strong enough by themselves. Marriage must be a cooperative effort recognizing the differences of male and female while at the same time allowing the interdependence to be celebrated and appreciated. From the very beginning Adam realized that after naming the living creatures that God created there was not a suitable or compatible helper for him. Two particular words (helper and suitable) in Genesis 2:18, "It is not good for man to be alone; I will make him a helper suitable for him" affirms the need and the design for equality intertwined with complementarity. "Through bearing the image of the divine, human relatedness was designed to be one of unity and equality within the framework of complementarity."[71] It is in the unity of the marriage covenant that male and female realize the purpose and character of God. This covenant is reciprocal and unconditional. The vows exchanged in the wedding ceremony, "for better or worse, for richer or poorer, in sickness and health, till death do us part" have unconditional commitment as the focus.

It is through the acknowledgement of the different gifts and attributes of male and female that marriages can truly "become one" as scripture declares. Complementarity is not an option but a command for the marriage context. We read in 1 Timothy 3:15, "may know how one ought to conduct himself in the household of God, which is the church of the living God"; as male and female

---

70 V. Norskov Olson. The New Relatedness for Man & Woman in Christ: A Mirror of the Divine. (Loma Linda, CA: Loma Linda University, 1993) p. 50.

71 Ibid., p. 44.

within the context of marriage and family, it is clear through the Word of God that there is a correct manner of behavior that is expected of the people of God. That behavior should edify the marriage covenant, the familial covenant and above all glorify God. I believe that true and effective marriages are built upon the fact that male and female were designed to work together, play together and raise a healthy family together utilizing the several gifts and attributes of both while acknowledging the beauty of their uniqueness. "In equal partnership marriages the locus of authority is placed in the relationship, not in one spouse or the other. Even though it may take longer to arrive at a joint decision, as the couple listens, honors and respects each other's opinion, they move toward a united stance."[72] Marriage if the desire is to be effective must be a partnership of equals. Creating a partnership takes time. It involves enduring many disappointments as well as many joys in the process.

Realizing mutual submission principles in the marital relationship requires patience. "Behind the "two are better than one" Scripture idea that two independent persons have unique strengths to offer each other and the relationship. Without two separate identities, interdependence is not possible."[73]

---

72 Ronald W. Pierce, Rebecca Merrill Groothuis, Gordon D. Fee., *Discovering Biblical Equality: Complementarity without Hierarchy.* (Downers Grove, IL: InterVarsity Press, 2004), p. 452.

73 Ibid., pg. 453.

PRE-MARITAL COUNSELING

*M*ulti-session pre-marital counseling is crucial in gaining the necessary tools to examine the many issues that enter in a marriage. A good marriage requires years of practical communication, and loving sensitivity. There must be a mutual submission, love and respect. Some issues that are often overlooked in marriages are: how to solve marital conflicts; how to manage money as a couple, or how to share holidays with your family of origin. For the most part, multi-session premarital counseling is useful and helpful. Couples should realize that these sessions help build trust and allow for the sharing of insights and help to devise a more personal wedding ceremony. These sessions also allow time for sharing family histories or genograms which allow for a deeper understanding of each other's familial system. It is also allows the couples to discover the importance of knowing their lives before the big wedding day. The information obtained in these sessions can prove to be helpful to the couple for years to come as well as help to flag areas that may need more work in the future.

Premarital counseling helps the couple to understand emotional triangles as well as the importance of knowing each other's roots. Additionally, these sessions help to identify and examine shared and differing values especially in the area of allegiance and closeness to nuclear family (immediate), approaches to dealing with money (spending and saving), family traditions (spoken and unspoken), the importance of sexual intimacy and expectations, communication, anger and conflict resolution approaches, expectation of marital roles and spousal authority, and the importance of romance.

Premarital counseling allows for redemptive conflict resolution and proactive approaches to problem solving. These sessions allow the minister to introduce to the couple "mentoring couples" who can share with them after the ceremony. Premarital counseling can help the couple build a solid foundation for sharing a lifetime of mutual respect and value for each other.

Marriage is about shared decision making, shared responsibility, shared intimacy, and shared fidelity, shared resources, and shared lives. A healthy marriage honors its vows and demonstrates mutual fidelity and respect.

The following ways are suggested for persons striving to model honor and respect within the marriage covenant:

- Speak with respect even through disagreements
- Offer constructive suggestions rather than destructive critiques
- Move from forcing an opinion toward consulting on an issue
- Lead from a "grace" perspective rather than a "power" perspective
- Speak in "I" messages and not "you" messages
- Reveal open and honest feelings and thoughts even when uncomfortable

- Listen in the moment without distractions from other sources

Strong marriages lead to stronger communities. Strong marriages allow us to be vulnerable with one another. I am convinced that as we grow as a couple, we are better equipped to be the presence of Christ in the lives of others.

PARENTHOOD

I now want to transition into my understanding of the nature of marriages as it relates to parenting. Marriage must include a desire to make it work. It must embrace the need to be complementary, fair and just. Likewise, marriages are more functional when a concerted effort at being effective parents is present. I have previously stated that there are no perfect families. There are no perfect marriages and therefore it stands to reason that there can not be a perfect way of raising children. Unfortunately when you begin to form a family based on the "American" dream of a spouse and 1.5 children, a white picket fence, a dog, cat and some gold fish, there usually is a reality check that needs to be acknowledged. Attending workshops, seminars and trainings may be helpful but should not be the only source of information. The information gleaned will be merely a scraping of the surface of what is in store for potential parents in any culture. Children don't come with instruction manuals nor do they come pre-wired to our expectations.

Parenthood on its best day can be a real mystery. It comes with lots of challenges, lots of joy, lots of tears and even more mistakes than most parents care to mention. When parenting, there must be a focus on fairness and trust in the familial relationships. It is necessary for parents to establish a solid foundation in which the children can gather helpful and life sustaining information to live out the biblical command and ultimately rest on the benefits of the commands contained in the Word of God. The edification of the children in the context of marriage and family should be the desired outcome of parents just as it is the desired outcome and end result of the gifts of the Spirit as proclaimed in Galatians 5:22-23, "but the fruit of the Spirit is love, joy, peace, longsuffering, kindness, goodness, faithfulness, gentleness, self-control, against such there is no law." These aforementioned traits will no doubt add to the tool box of parents as they instill them in their children.

There are hundreds if not thousands of books that claim to capture the "right way" of parenting in today's society. Similarly, there are many parenting styles to consider including: authoritarian, permissive, and assertive-democratic. An authoritarian style tends to be more rigid. It commands the child to do certain things without bending the rules. A permissive style tends to be more hands-off in its approach. This style allows the children to learn from their mistakes. The assertive-democratic parent tends to establish basic guidelines and clarity while allowing the children a voice and a vote in the process. These parenting styles along with others should be considered when approaching a theology for marriage and family. "An age-old debate centers on permissive parenting versus restrictive parenting. Permissive parents recognize the importance of warmth, affection, and emotional security, but downplay discipline. Restrictive parents, on the other hand, emphasize discipline, responsibility, and self-control, but pay less attention to emotional bonding and nurture."[74] Scripture instructs parents to develop or train up a child in the way that they should go (Proverbs 22:6). I believe parenting is a monumental responsibility and requires all the resources available to ensure a well-balanced and healthy child. "The complementary nature of shared parenting means children receive different strengths from each parent. When one parent needs relief, a second parent can be fully present and connected with the child." [75] Effective parenting requires the skills and the patience of both parents. I believe shared or complementary parenting tends to strengthen the marriage and ultimately leads to a healthy family. This style of parenting leads to a more balanced family; a family that spends quality time together, a family that enjoys eating meals at the dinner table at the same time, a family that enjoys traveling together and doing those memorable things that create a lasting legacy. I would imagine the desired outcome for any parent is to parent effectively with the information they have learned. Understanding the complexities of parenting will help to navigate the sometimes challenging and difficult experiences, as well as allow for appreciation of the journey called parenting. A well functioning family is engaged in mutual reciprocity of care, consideration and interdependence. As I reflect on growing up and being parented, I recall my mother sharing with me the following poem that helped me to gain a greater appreciation for being in a family. This poem by Langston Hughes demonstrates the need to navigate the pitfalls of parenting and at the same time appreciate the joy of parenting. It is entitled: "Mother to Son"

74　Judy and Jack Balswick, Don and Boni Piper. *Relationship-Empowerment Parenting: Building Formative and Fulfilling Relationships with your Children.* (Grand Rapids, MI: Baker Books, 2003), p. 18.

75　Ibid., p. 28.

Well son, I'll tell you:
Life for me ain't been no crystal stair, It's had tacks in
it, and splinters, and boards torn up, and places with no
carpet on the floor,
    Bare; But all the time, I'se been climbin on, and
reachin; landins, and turnin corners, And sometimes
going in the dark, where there ain't been no light. So boy,
don't you turn back; Don't you set down on the steps
    'Cause you find it's kinder hard, Don't you fall now
– For I'se still goin, honey, I'se still climbin, And Life for
me ain't been no crystal stair.

When parenting, I have found it useful to see the family as a system, a whole entity in need of valuing and honoring all members of the family. For example, if you were to enter a baking contest and your "prize winning" cake or family were to be dissected to determine each individual ingredient used, you may find that some of the components may not taste so good by themselves, however, when combined and borrowing from its specific uniqueness, apply the necessary heat and pressure, you eventually end up with a "prize winning" cake, or in other words, a well functioning family. It is also helpful for the parent to model what they are teaching or instructing their children. One sure way of creating havoc in a family is for a child to see their parent engaging in activity that was previously forbidden or at least frowned upon. This type of lifestyle as viewed from the eyes of a child tends to be hypocritical and suspect for future teaching moments; in other words, parents should walk the talk and exhibit a lifestyle that is worthy of emulation by their children. "The old adage that what children learn is caught and not taught applies here. Research shows that modeling is one of the most effective ways to inculcate values and desired behavior in children." [76] I believe invisible

---

76 Ibid., p. 25.

loyalties can be experienced here. The loyalty expectations can either free or cause bondage.

"The criteria for parenting in the contemporary world are under heated discussion. And in the nuclear family itself, marriage is often unstable. New forms of parenting, eg., divorce, single parenting and remarriage, create new challenges to continuity and security."[77] Parenting can present adults with a source of gratification and even accomplishment. It can also be quite a responsibility. This is true of two parent households or single parent households. The absence of one of the parents compounds the complexity and developmental burdens of the single parent. "Inclinations to abandon parental responsibility are not a new phenomenon. What is new is the absence of a kinship system that might protect the members of a family when its nuclear structure begins to break up."[78] I know first hand the difficulties that a single parent must endure in raising their children. Feelings of helplessness, hopelessness and even failure are often themes that a single parent faces. Conversely, feelings of joy and satisfaction are also present themes especially when the child becomes an adult and the single parent can see the fruits of their labor.

In our attempts to be good parents we must consider the following assumptions as stated in Anderson & Guerney's "On Being Family" first, creatureliness is a necessary but insufficient condition for human existence; second, human existence is originally social and only consequentially psychological; third, existence as a person derives from existence in relation; finally, human being, as differentiated from no-human creatureliness, is being that is characterized by openness toward the power that constitutes it. Our

---

77   Ivan Boszormenyi-Nagy & Barbara R. Krasner *Between Give and Take: A Clinical Guide to Contextual Therapy.* (New York: Brunner/Mazel Publishers, 1986)., p. 356.

78   Ibid., p. 359.

children will be best served if we acknowledge the aforementioned assumptions. "The parent, however, summons the latent mystery of the "I" into relation, which is a summons into responsibility into communion. Thus parenting is necessarily humanizing when it takes place under the divine commandment, while educating may or may not be."[79] Finally, a poem written by Dorothy Law Nolte, tends to sum up the notion that children can be what God designed them to be if given the proper instruction, the unconditional love and the godly guidance parents are designed to exhibit before their children.

The poem is entitled:

"Children Learn What They Live."
If children live with criticism, they learn to condemn.
If children live with hostility, they learn to fight.
If children live with fear, they learn to be apprehensive.
If children live with pity, they learn to feel sorry for themselves.
If children live with ridicule, they learn to feel shy.
If children live with jealousy, they learn to feel envy.
If children live with shame, they learn to feel guilty.
If children live with encouragement, they learn confidence.
If children live with tolerance, they learn patience.
If children live with praise, they learn appreciation.
If children live with acceptance, they learn to love.
If children live with approval, they learn to like themselves.
If children live with recognition, they learn it is good to have a goal.
If children live with sharing, they learn generosity.
If children live with honesty, they learn truthfulness.

---

79   Ray S. Anderson & Dennis B. Guernsey. *On Being Family: A Social Theology of the Family.* (Grand Rapids, MI: Eerdmans, 1985), p. 60.

If children live with fairness, they learn justice.
If children live with kindness and consideration, they learn respect.
If children live with security, they learn to have faith in themselves and in those about them.
If children live with friendliness, they learn the world is a nice place in which to live.

Lastly, the task of parenting should be done in a manner that will prepare the child for the complex world that awaits them. If the desired outcome is to prepare a child by providing a loving and safe environment than I am convinced that successful parenting can be performed by a two parent household or a single parent household. "Parenting, therefore, is the arena in which the human person learns the necessary skills to function as an adult – whether married or single. In that sense and for that reason we begin with parenting in our developmental model."[80]

---

80 Ibid., p.82.

DIVORCE AND ITS CONSEQUENCES

"*All was well in the* Garden of Eden, until Adam and Eve chose self-gratification over obedience to God. From that point the history of humanity has been littered with examples of what it meant to "fall"."[81] Statistics have shown that all marriages do not honor the vows of the covenant nor are they always healthy or safe. "We tend to think of divorce as a single event in people's lives. Nothing could be further from the truth. Separation and divorce set in motion a chain of events that spans an extended period of time."[82] "Human nature is no different today than it was thirty years ago and yet thirty years ago, most people got married, stayed married. Today, most fail, and an increasing number never even try."[83] If a couple should find themselves in

---

81   John P. Splinter. *The Complete Divorce Recovery Handbook*. Grand Rapids, MI: Zondervan Publishing House. 1992., p. 187.

82   Genevieve Clapp. *Divorce & New Beginnings: A Complete Guide to Recovery, Solo Parenting, Co-Parenting, and Stepfamilies*. New York, NY: 2000., 4.

83   Maggie Gallagher. The Abolition of Marriage: How We Destroy Lasting Love. Washington, D.C.: Regenery Publishing, Inc., 1996., p. 10.

a relationship that is not healthy or safe, divorce is often sought. Divorce can be a devastating reality for all concerned, especially for the children if they are present. Divorce has the potential of physical violence, and economic depravation.

"Middle-class security is the most obvious casualty of marriage's collapse. Single moms are five times more likely to be poor than their married sisters."[84] The evidence is now over whelming that he collapse of marriage is creating a whole generation of children less happy, less physically and mentally healthy, less equipped to deal with life or to produce at work, and more dangerous to themselves and others."[85] Children of divorce often find themselves in disciplinary problems merely seeking attention from their once married parents. There are many intergenerational consequences that will be felt by families of divorce. At a minimum, there is the need for transition both physically and emotionally. There is the task of rebuilding your self-esteem and self-worth. Additionally, there will be periods of coping with loneliness and building of a new social support network. "Most people think of divorce adjustments as coping with the divorce itself – weathering the stormy emotions, dealing with the disruptions and problems, helping children adjust, and learning to let go."[86] There are other examples of brokenness that can cause a couple to seek divorce. "Historically, western law has specified four kinds of grounds that would permit divorce: adultery, mental cruelty, desertion, and nonconsumation."[87]

---

84 Ibid., p. 31.

85 Ibid., p.34.

86 Genevieve Clapp. *Divorce & New Beginnings: A Complete Guide to Recovery, Solo Parenting, Co-Parenting, and Stepfamilies.* New York, NY: 2000., p.161.

87 Joy K. Rice & David G. Rice. *Living Through Divorce: A Developmental Approach to Divorce Therapy.* New York, NY: The Guilford Press.1986., p. 10.

"Following the decision to divorce and its implementation, initial relief or elation often is followed by renewed distress, depression, and the loss of self-esteem."[88] Divorce brings about many emotions and feelings. Sadness, grief and even anger can be present for undetermined amounts of time. It is important for persons going through divorce to seek outside professional help and support groups to gain the tools necessary for the healing process. The mere fact of all the adjustments needed during and after a divorce can be overwhelming to all concerned. "Too many simultaneous stresses can produce significant overload and the therapist can help the client assess what situational changes must be made immediately and what can wait until the gradual return of amore normal mood and elevated confidence."[89]

Additional examples of brokenness in the marriage are physical abuse. "Of all the risks of the collapse of marriage, perhaps the most horrifying and the least remarked is child abuse. Ironically, violence and abuse are routinely used to indict marriage and justify the divorce revolution."[90] There are a number of ways to be supportive of families that experience divorce. One way is to provide emotional support through small group or peer-group sessions. Another way is to help build up their self-esteem and demonstrate that a marriage collapse is not always the fault of one person. Another way is to provide structured educational opportunities for both the adults and the children. These opportunities would be designed to help all concerned distinguish the difference between forgiveness and exoneration. It would provide a sense of accountability and culpability for the collapse of the marriage.

88 Ibid., p. 170.
89 Ibid., p. 172.
90 Maggie Gallagher. The Abolition of Marriage: How We Destroy Lasting Love. Washington, D.C.: Regenery Publishing, Inc., 1996., p. 36.

Over the last several decades, our culture has become very casual about accepting divorce and has created a social climate where divorce is viewed as an easy way to get out of one's commitments. Couples seem to be much less likely nowadays to work through the tough times in their relationship than they were twenty or thirty years ago because divorce is relatively easy — legally speaking — and is accepted as perfectly fine behavior. Not every divorce has the same circumstances surrounding it and not everyone who gets divorced does so out of a lack of commitment or failure in understanding the seriousness of the marriage covenant. That being said, the truth is that many, many people today do indeed take the whole institution of marriage way too lightly.

Now, I want to caution you at this point: Don't misunderstand what I'm saying, or get only part of picture. I'm not saying that all marriages fail simply because people lack the commitment to work through problems. I'm not even saying that every marriage ought to be saved. Certainly the wife whose husband is physically abusive to her or her children should never stay with him. Even if divorce is ultimately not in order, church leaders should never be the ones telling a woman to go back to the man when doing so puts her or the children in harm's way! Get out of there, now! It should be unthinkable to the Christian to try and send her back.

So, no, divorce is not okay. It is sometimes justifiable, more often it is inevitable; but it is most certainly not "okay." Our marriage was such smooth sailing, relatively speaking, that my heart really goes out to people who have had cope with the fact that their closest, most personal of all relationships has gone sour. A husband or wife is supposed to be the person who is our refuge against the storms of life. They are to comfort us, help us cope with all the garbage that life just naturally throws at us. When that relationship is part of what's wrong with one's life, it can be overwhelming. And that is precisely why we must remember that God does indeed hate divorce, but He does not hate divorced people. When a marriage fails, is a tragedy. It is a failure; there is some sin involved. The truth is that we are all failures in certain areas of our lives. I seriously doubt that any of us can claim to have reached perfection. Yes, we have been cleansed from sin, but we still live with sin's short-term consequences. Keeping this in mind, Christians must have open hearts and minds, as well as reach out in love to those who are hurting because of divorce.

Spiritually speaking, the person going through a divorce is usually in critical condition. They feel worthless because the man or woman they once loved above all others is no longer a part of their lives. They probably feel that they cannot do anything right. They can't imagine a good future for themselves or their children. They have a serious need for real friendship. And they have real needs in taking care of practical, everyday problems.

As I said, my heart goes out to people in these situations. Just as we are in many other areas, are called by God, in this area of divorce, to both uphold and strive for a biblical understanding of import and duration of the marriage covenant. It's a special relationship, unlike all other earthly relationships. It shouldn't be entered into lightly nor dissolved on a whim. In fact, Jesus says that ideally it should last until death. We have to uphold that ideal, because the Bible teaches it.

Concluding Thoughts

As I bring this book to a close, I am reminded that as a child I would often put together model airplanes or model cars. It was not until nearly hours and possibly weeks that I discovered after reading the instruction manual that I was missing a few essential parts to complete my project or task. At first glance, the model looked as it should, the colors and the decals were properly placed, the glue dried without a mess but ultimately something was still missing. Well, that's how I feel about this paper. From the outside, it looks fine, but after careful inspection, even after hundreds of hours reading and digesting material and data, I still feel that something may well be missing. The instruction books have been read but I feel like I did when I was putting together that model airplane or model car, something seems to be missing. Having said that, I pray that what has been read thus far will prove to be a strong foundation for moving toward a theology of marriage and family, recognizing that something may be missing, primarily because this is a work in progress.

Finally, I believe I have captured to the best of my ability the essence and the meaning of contextual therapy as it stands side by side with theology. The ethical perspective present within contextual therapy combined with the teachings of the Word of God is sure to be a lasting and firm foundation in which to build a healthy and well functioning marriage and family. The healthy understanding and application of family legacies, the invisible loyalties, the indebtedness, the entitlement and the ledgers identified in contextual therapy can truly bring about a sense of harmony in the family of origin as well as the family of procreation. This can be brought about if all parties are intentional and deliberate in understanding the blessings and the curses that are present and may be lying dormant within their families.

When these components are recognized and applied families will be able to maneuver around the imbalances that are a by product of their family of origin. With this understanding, family members will be valued and will have a sense of relatedness and a source of strength from within the family. They will be accountable to each other as they assess the patterns observed with their family and balance their behavior in a more effective and healthy manner.

WORKS CITED

Anderson Ray S., and Guernsey, Dennis B. On Being Family: A Social Theology of the Family: Grand Rapids, MI: Eerdmans, 1985

The Book of Discipline of The United Methodist Church. (Nashville, TN: United Methodist Publishing House, 2004)

Balswick, Judith & Balswick, Jack O. Authentic Human Sexuality: An Integrated Christian Approach. Downers Grove, IL: Intervarsity Press, 1999.

Balswick, Judy and Jack, Piper, Don and Boni. Relationship-Empowerment Parenting: Building Formative and Fulfilling Relationships with your Children. Grand Rapids, MI: Baker Books, 2003.

Becvar Dorothy Stroh, and Becvar, Raphel J., Family Therapy: A Systemic Integration. Pearson Education Publishing: Needham Heights, MA, 2000.

Boszormenyi-Nagy, Ivan and Spark, Geraldine M. Invisibile Loyalties: Reciprocity In Intergenerational Family Therapy. NewYork: Brunner/Mazel Publishers, 1984.

Boszormenyi-Nagy, Ivan & Krasner, Barbara R. Between Give and Take: A Clinical Guide to Contextual Therapy. New York: Brunner/Mazel Publishers, 1986.

Brauch, Manfred. Handout entitled: The Biblical Ideal of Exclusiveness and Permanence in the Male-Female Relation of Marriage. Palmer Theological Seminary, January 12, 2007.

Browning, Don S. Religious Thought and the Modern Psychologies. Philadelphia, PA: Fortress Press, 1987.

Captain, Philip A. Eight Stages of Christian Growth: Human Development in Psycho-Spiritual Terms. New Jersey: Prentice-Hall, Inc., 1984.

Carter, John D., Narramore, Bruce. The Integration of Psychology and Theology: An Introduction. Grand Rapids, Michigan: Zondervan Corporation. 1979.

Clapp, Genevieve. Divorce & New Beginnings: A Complete Guide to Recovery , Solo Parenting, Co-Parenting, and Stepfamilies. New York, NY: 2000.

Erickson, Erik H., Identity and the Life Cycle. New York: W.W. Norton & Company, 1980.

Fee, Gordon D., Stuart, Douglas. How to Read the Bible for all its Worth: A Guide to Understanding the Bible. Grand Rapids, Michigan: Zondervan Publishing House, 1993

Fowler, James W., Becoming Adult, Becoming Christian: Adult Development & Christian Faith. San Francisco, CA: Jossey-Bass Publishers, 2000.

Gallagher, Maggie. The Abolition of Marriage: How We Destroy Lasting Love. Washington, D.C.: Regenery Publishing, Inc., 1996.

Goldenberg, Irene and Goldenberg, Herbert. Family Therapy: An Overview, Sixth Edition Pacific Grove, CA: Brooks/Cole Thomson, 2004

Gorsuch, Richard L. Integrating Psychology and Spirituality? Praeger Publishing: Westport, Connecticut, 2002.

Gushee, David P., Getting Marriage Right: Realistic Counsel for Saving & Strengthening Relationships. Grand Rapids, MI: Baker Books, 2004.

Hecker, Lorna L., Wetchler, Joseph L. An Introduction to Marriage and Family Therapy (New York: Haworth Press, 2003.

Heusden, Ammy van, Eerenbeemt, ElseMarie van den. Balance in Motion: Ivan Boszormenyi-Nagy and His Vision of Individual and Family Therapy. New York: Brunner/Mazel Publishers, 1987.

Kramer, Jeannette R. Family Interfaces: Transgenerational Patterns. New York: Brunner/Mazel Publishers, 1985.

Olson, V. Norskov. The New Relatedness for Man & Woman in Christ: A Mirror of the Divine. Loma Linda, CA: Loma Linda University, 1993.

Pierce, Ronald W., Merrill Groothuis, Rebecca, Fee, Gordon D. Discovering Biblical Equality: Complementarity without Hierarchy. Downers Grove, IL: InterVarsity Press, 2004

Rabin, Albert I. Psychological Issues in Biblical Lore: Explorations in the Old Testament. New York: Springer Publishing Company, 1998.

Rice, Joy K. & Rice, David G. Living Through Divorce: A Developmental Approach to Divorce Therapy. New York, NY: The Guilford Press.1986.,

Salkind., Neil J. Theories of Human Development. New York: Litton Educational Publishing. 1981.

Schreck., G. Peter. Handout entitled: Personhood and Relational Life Tasks: A Model for Integrating Psychology and Theology. January 2007 Intensive, Palmer Theological Seminary, p. 78.

Splinter, John P. The Complete Divorce Recovery Handbook. Grand Rapids, MI: Zondervan Publishing House. 1992.,

Stevenson, Daryl H., Eck, Brian E., Hill, Peter C. <u>Psychology & Christianity Integration: Seminal Works that Shaped the Movement</u>. Batavia, Illinois: Christian Association for Psychological Studies, Inc. 2007.

Tetlow, Elisabeth Meier and Tetlow, Louis Mulry. <u>Partners in Service: Toward a Biblical Theology of Christian Marriage</u>. Lanham, MD: University Press, 1983.

Van Leeuwen, Mary Stewart. <u>The Person in Psychology</u>. Grand Rapids, MI: William B. Eerdmans Publishing Company, 1985.